Conserving the
Nature of America

The mission of the U.S. Fish and Wildlife Service is working with others to conserve, protect, and enhance fish, wildlife, plants and their habitats for the continuing benefit of the American people.

Who We Are...

A Conservation Legacy
The U.S. Fish and Wildlife Service is the only agency of the U.S. Government whose primary responsibility is fish, wildlife, and plant conservation.

The Service helps protect a healthy environment for people, fish and wildlife, and helps Americans conserve and enjoy the outdoors and our living treasures. The Service's major responsibilities are for migratory birds, endangered species, certain marine mammals, and freshwater and anadromous fish.

Over 125 Years of Service
The Service's origins date back to 1871, when Congress established the U.S. Fish Commission to study the decrease of the nation's food fishes and recommend ways to reverse the decline. Meanwhile, in 1885, Congress created an Office of Economic Ornithology in the Department of Agriculture. The office studied the food habits and migratory patterns of birds, especially those that had an effect on agriculture. This office gradually grew in responsibilities and went through several name changes until finally renamed the Bureau of Biological Survey in 1905.

In addition to studying birds and mammals, the Survey's responsibilities included managing the nation's first wildlife refuges, controlling predators, enforcing wildlife laws, and conserving

Mallard
USFWS Photo by:
Erwin & Peggy Bauer

Brown Bear
USFWS Photo by:
Larry Aumiller

dwindling populations of migratory birds. The Bureaus of Fisheries and Biological Survey were transferred to the Department of the Interior in 1939. In 1940, they were combined and named the Fish and Wildlife Service.

Further reorganization came in 1956 when the Fish and Wildlife Act created the United States Fish and Wildlife Service and established two bureaus, Sport Fish and Wildlife and Commercial Fisheries. In 1970, the Bureau of Commercial Fisheries was transferred to the Department of Commerce and renamed the National Marine Fisheries Service.

For many years the Service was the principal federal wildlife and fisheries research agency. In the 1940's, Service research biologists conducted some of the first investigations into the effects of the pesticide DDT in wildlife. Service researchers also revealed the life cycle of the parasite that causes whirling disease in trout. In addition, Service biologists developed many of the captive breeding techniques that have benefitted such rare species as whooping cranes, California condors and black-footed ferrets. The Service's research function briefly became an independent agency and was eventually reorganized as part of the U.S. Geological Survey in 1996.

Notable former employees include Jay N. "Ding" Darling, designer of the first Federal Duck Stamp, and Rachel Carson, author of *Silent Spring*.

Today, the Service employs approximately 7,500 people at facilities across the country including a headquarters office in Washington, D.C., seven regional offices, and nearly 700 field units. Among these are national wildlife refuges, national fish hatcheries and management assistance offices, law enforcement and ecological services field stations.

Wood Duck
USFWS Photo by:
Maslowski Photo

What We Do...

Over 500 National Wildlife Refuges

The National Wildlife Refuge System is the world's largest and most diverse collection of lands set aside specifically for wildlife. The refuge system began in 1903, when President Theodore Roosevelt designated 3-acre Pelican Island, a pelican and heron rookery in Florida, as a bird sanctuary. Today, more than 500 National Wildlife Refuges have been established from the Arctic Ocean to the South Pacific, from Maine to the Caribbean. Varying in size from half-acre parcels to thousands of square miles, they encompass more than 93 million acres of America's best wildlife habitats. The vast majority of these lands are in Alaska, with the rest spread across the United States and several U.S. territories.

Migratory Bird Conservation

Because many bird species fly thousands of miles in their annual migrations, they cannot be effectively conserved by any single state or nation, but only through cooperative efforts. The Fish and Wildlife Service is responsible for migratory bird conservation under several laws and international treaties with Canada, Mexico, Japan, and the former Soviet Union. This includes the conservation of more than 800 species of migratory birds. The Service regulates migratory bird hunting and studies populations. It also monitors and promotes the conservation of songbirds and other nongame species.

Biological Expertise

The Fish and Wildlife Service provides expert biological advice to other federal agencies, states, industry, Native American tribes and members of the public concerning the conservation of fish, wildlife, and plant habitat that may be affected by development activities. Working through field offices located throughout the country, Service personnel assess the potential effects of projects that require federal funding

Okefenokee NWR
USFWS Photo by:
George Gentry

or permits, such as dredge and fill activities, dams and reservoirs, oil leasing, energy projects, and federal highways. Service biologists recommend ways to avoid, minimize, or compensate for harmful impacts on fish and wildlife resources. Service personnel also assess the effects of contaminants on fish and wildlife.

Fish Conservation and Restoration

One of the U.S. Fish and Wildlife Service's most important duties is to conserve populations of fish and other aquatic species, and to protect and restore the habitats these species need. Service fisheries biologists, operating from a nationwide network of Fish and Wildlife Management Assistance Offices, National Fish Hatcheries, Fish Technology Centers, and Fish Health Centers, have a wealth of expertise in aquatic resource conservation. Through its efforts, the U.S. Fish and Wildlife Service helps safeguard fisheries worth billions of dollars, rescues troubled aquatic species on the brink of extinction, and provides opportunities for anglers and others to enjoy the outdoors.

Newly Hatched Salmon
USFWS Photo

Endangered Species Recovery

Another major function of the Fish and Wildlife Service is the identification and protection of endangered species. About 1,200 domestic species are currently on the federal list of endangered and threatened species. As part of their responsibilities, Service biologists work with scientists

Striped Bass
USFWS Photo by:
Ashton Graham

from other federal and state agencies, universities, Native American tribes and private organizations to develop "recovery plans" that identify actions needed to save listed species and restore their numbers. Recovery programs may include research, habitat preservation and management, captive breeding, law enforcement, reintroduction of depleted species into suitable areas of their historic range, and other activities.

Conserving Ecosystems

Through its "ecosystem approach" adopted in 1994, the Service works to achieve landscape-level conservation of fish, wildlife, plants, and their habitats through coordination among all Service programs and field stations, and through partnerships with other agencies, organizations and individuals. The Service identified 53 ecosystem units based on U.S. Geological Survey watersheds and has established teams to address important conservation issues in each ecosystem.

Co-op Farming
USFWS Photo by:
Karen Hollingsworth

Partnerships

The Partners for Fish and Wildlife program works with private landowners who want to restore fish and wildlife habitat. Since 1987, the Service has established nearly 20,000 cooperative agreements with private land owners to restore habitat on private land. So far, partners in the program have restored more than 400,000 acres of wetlands, 300,000 acres of native prairie and grassland, and 2,000 miles of stream-side corridors. In recent years, the Service has maintained a waiting list of

Mexican Wolf
USFWS Photo by:
Jim Clark

Monarch on Common Milkweed, Edwin B. Forsythe NWR
USFWS Photo by: Karen Hollingsworth

approximately 2,000 landowners nationwide interested in this cost-shared program.

Working Around the World

The Service conserves fish and wildlife worldwide under some 40 treaties, statutes, and agreements. The Service also cooperates with other countries on wildlife research and management programs, and responds to requests from foreign countries for technical assistance. The Service's goal is to help cooperating countries develop their conservation capabilities in order to meet their own environmental goals and needs on a sustainable basis. Among the Service's international programs are graduate education programs for fish and wildlife managers in Latin America, environmental education in the Near East, Asia, Africa, and Latin America, and special conservation efforts for tigers, rhinoceroses, and African elephants.

The Service also works with other countries to preserve their native wildlife and plants through the Convention on International Trade in Endangered Species of Wild Fauna and Flora (CITES). The United States is one of more than 145 countries that now belong to this international treaty aimed at preventing overexploitation of rare wildlife from commercial trade.

Law Enforcement

The Service's Law Enforcement operations support the entire range of its wildlife conservation programs.

Illegal Wildlife Products
USFWS Photo by: Carl Zitzmann

Service special agents and wildlife inspectors enforce wildlife laws and treaty obligations. Special agents investigate cases ranging from individual migratory bird hunting violations to large-scale poaching and illegal trafficking in protected wildlife. Working in cooperation with U.S. Customs and Department of Agriculture inspectors, Service wildlife inspectors monitor wildlife trade and stop illegal shipments of protected plants and animals. The Service operates the world's most comprehensive wildlife forensics laboratory, where Service experts analyze evidence to help investigators solve wildlife crimes.

Checking Hunting License
USFWS Photo by:
Tupper Blake

Helping Tribes, States and Citizens

In accordance with its 1994 Native American policy, the Service maintains a government to government relationship and observes federal trust responsibilities with the Indian community. Through cooperative agreements, memoranda of understanding, and other relationships, the Service works with Native American tribes to help conserve wolves and other species, operate fish hatcheries, and manage migratory birds. In all its programs, the Service strives to respect the cultural values of the

Fishing - Help Our Kids Catch a Dream
USFWS Photo by:
Carl Zitzmann

Indian community and recognize the individuality and sovereignty of each Indian nation.

Two additional laws administered by the Fish and Wildlife Service — the Federal Aid in Wildlife Restoration Act and the Federal Aid in Sport Fish Restoration Act — provide federal grant money to support specific projects carried out by state fish and wildlife agencies. The money comes from federal excise taxes paid by hunters, anglers and boaters on sporting arms and ammunition, archery equipment, sport fishing tackle, motorboat fuels and import duties on fishing tackle and pleasure boats.

Partnerships Yield Greater Benefits for All
USFWS Photo by: Ryan Hagerty

States use the funds to acquire land for wildlife habitat and for fishing and other recreation; conduct research; provide access to hunting, fishing, and boating areas; manage and maintain fish and wildlife habitats; and carry out hunting safety training and aquatic education.

Career Opportunities
Working for the Fish and Wildlife Service is more than a career. It is also a commitment—one shared by more than 7,500 men and women representing a wide range of professions, trades, and specialties. To accomplish its mission, the Service employs many of the country's best biologists, wildlife managers, engineers, realty specialists, law enforcement

Sandhill Crane Colt
USFWS Photo by: William Radke

agents, and others working to assure that future generations of Americans will be able to enjoy nature's beauty and bounty. For information on working for the Service, contact the Regional office nearest you.

Louisiana Black Bear Research
USFWS Photo by:
Mark Chesna

Opportunities for the Public

Thousands of Americans volunteer with the Service each year. Working side-by-side with Service employees, volunteers serve as tour guides and educators and help with management activities such as bird banding, habitat restoration, wildlife population surveys, building trails, and staffing visitor centers. Many citizens also join "Friends" groups that support national wildlife refuges in their community. There are also many opportunities for citizens to comment on major Service actions and the development of management plans for Service facilities. To learn more, check our web site or contact a Service office near you.

Volunteer on Refuge
USFWS Photo by:
Karen Hollingsworth

Big Horned Sheep
USFWS Photo by:
Karen Hollingsworth

Laws We Carry Out

The Fish and Wildlife Service administers and enforces a number of conservation laws and treaties. Among them are:

- The Lacey Act, (1900) which prohibits the interstate or international shipment of illegally taken wildlife.

Law Enforcement
USFWS Photo by:
Karen Hollingsworth

- The Migratory Bird Treaty Act, (1918) which bans the take, possession, purchase, sale, or barter of any migratory bird, including feathers, parts, nests, or eggs.

- The Migratory Bird Hunting and Conservation Stamp Act, (1934) which requires all waterfowl hunters age 16 and over to possess a Federal Duck Stamp.

Northern Flicker
USFWS Photo by:
Denny Bingaman

- The Federal Aid in Wildlife Restoration Act, (1937) which provides Federal excise taxes on hunting equipment to state fish and wildlife agencies for restoration of wild birds and animals; acquisition, development and management of wildlife habitats; hunter education and development and management of shooting ranges.

- The Eagle Protection Act, (1940) which prohibits the import, export, take, sale, purchase, or barter of bald and golden eagles.

Red Wolf Pups
USFWS Photo by:
George Gentry

- The Federal Aid in Sport Fish Restoration Act, (1950) which provides federal excise taxes on fishing and boating equipment to state fish and wildlife agencies for sport fish management, boating access, and aquatic education projects.

- The Endangered Species Act, (1973) which provides for the listing, protection and recovery of endangered and threatened fish, wildlife and plants.

Sandhill Cranes,
Bosque del Apache
USFWS Photo by:
Virginia Heitman

- The Marine Mammal Protection Act, (1972) which establishes a moratorium on the taking and importing of marine mammals, such as sea otter, walrus, polar bear, dugong, and manatee.

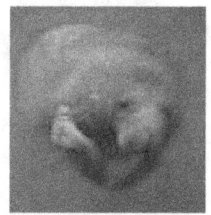

Manatee
USFWS Photo by:
James Powell

- The Convention on International Trade in Endangered Species of Wild Fauna and Flora (CITES), (1975) which regulates the importation, exportation, and re-exportation of thousands of species protected under its three appendices.

- The Wild Bird Conservation Act, (1992) which addresses problems with the international trade in wild-caught birds.

Seized Cockatoos
USFWS Photo by:
Steve Hillebrand

- The National Wildlife Refuge System Improvement Act, (1997) which establishes wildlife conservation as the fundamental mission of the refuge system. The Act also recognizes wildlife-dependent recreational uses involving hunting, fishing, wildlife observation and photography, and environmental education and interpretation as the priority public uses of the Refuge System.

Environmental Education
USFWS Photo by:
Karen Hollingsworth

Why We Do It... **Conserving the Nature of America**
The U.S. Fish and Wildlife Service
helps protect a healthy environment
for people, fish and wildlife, and
helps Americans conserve and enjoy
the outdoors.

American Toad
USFWS Photo by:
Karen Hollingsworth

Wildlife Observation
USFWS Photo by: Karen Hollingsworth

Canoeing on Refuge
USFWS Photo by: Ryan Hagerty

Pelicans at Sunset
USFWS Photo by: George Gentry

Bluebells
USFWS Photo by: Jim Clark

Waterfowl Hunting
USFWS Photo by: Mike Hemming

*Conservation
is for Today
and the Future*
USFWS Photo by:
Carl Zitzmann

Hawksbill Sea Turtle
USFWS Photo by: Anja Burns

For More Information

Where We Are

**U.S. Fish & Wildlife Service
Headquarters
U.S. Department of the Interior**
1849 C Street, NW
Washington, DC 22040
202/208 5634
www.fws.gov

Pacific Region
911 NE 11th Avenue
Portland, Oregon 97232 - 4181
503/231 6121

*CA, HI, ID, NV,
OR, WA, and
Pacific islands*

Southwest Region
500 Gold Avenue, SW Room 3018
Albuquerque, New Mexico 87102
505/248 6911

AZ, NM, OK, TX

Great Lakes - Big Rivers Region
Federal Building - 1 Federal Drive
Fort Snelling, Minnesota 55111 - 4056
612/713 5360

*IL, IN, IA, MI,
MN, MO, OH, WI*

Southeast Region
1875 Century Boulevard, Suite 410
Atlanta, Georgia 30345
404/679 7289

*AL, AR, FL, GA,
KY, LA, MS, NC,
SC, TN, PR, VI*

Northeast Region
300 Westgate Center Drive
Hadley, Massachusetts 01035 - 9589
413/253 8322

*CT, DE, DC, ME,
MD, MA, NH,
NJ, NY, PA, RI,
VT, VA, WV*

Mountain - Prairie Region
134 Union Boulevard
Lakewood, Colorado 80228
303/236 7905

*CO, KS, MT, NE,
ND, SD, UT, WY*

Alaska Region
1011 East Tudor Road
Anchorage, Alaska 99503
907/786 3309

AK

To reach any of the Regional Offices
go to: *http://offices.fws.gov*

Sandhill Crane
USFWS Photo by:
Tupper Blake